W9-AKC-243

Peekaboo

and Other Games to Play with Your Baby

Tools for Everyday Parenting Series

by Shari Steelsmith
Illustrated by Rebekah Strecker

Parenting Press, Inc.
Seattle, Washington

Dedicated to all my grandmothers: Irene, Charlotte, and Jane

ISBN 0-943990-81-5 Paperback
ISBN 0-943990-99-8 Library binding

Cover and text design by Cameron Mason
Cover illustration by Karen Anne Pew

Library of Congress Cataloging-in-Publication Data
Steelsmith, Shari
     Peekaboo, and other games to play with your baby / by Shari Steelsmith ; illustrated by Rebekah Strecker.
        p.   cm. -- (Tools for everyday parenting series)
     Includes bibliographical references and index.
     ISBN 0-943990-99-8. -- ISBN 0-943990-81-5 (pbk.)
     1. Infants--Development. 2. Play. 3. Games. I. Strecker, Rebekah. II. Title. III. Title: Peekaboo. IV. Series.
HQ774.S813   1994
649' . 122--dc20
                                                                94-23011
                                                                CIP

Parenting Press, Inc.
P.O. Box 75267
Seattle, Washington 98125

Contents

Introduction

Babies like to play, and it's fun to play with them. Playing is how babies learn. When they play, they use their five senses: sight, sound (language), touch (movement), taste, and smell. Even very young babies learn this way. Parents can give them lots of chances to play and learn.

This book offers you many ideas for simple ways to play with babies of all ages.

Playing with Your Baby

When you play with your baby, she responds by making a face, smiling, or waving her hands and feet. Praise her when she responds. Clap your hands, kiss her, hug her, or use words, *"Good! You like this game."*

If your baby acts bored or fussy, stop playing. You can try the game again some other time. She will enjoy and learn from play only if she is ready for it.

Your baby can also get fussy and confused if too much is going on around her. There may be too much noise, or too many people around for her to pay attention to the game. You can tell if your baby feels this way if she does some of these things: clenches her fists, purses her lips, curls her toes, squirms a lot, looks away, sneezes, or yawns.

Differences in Children

Not all babies are the same. The game that your baby likes will probably be different from the game your friend's baby likes. Or maybe your baby will respond differently than you expect. That's okay. Don't try to make your baby play something she doesn't like. You can change the game a little bit, or try another game. She may not want to play at all. Be gentle and ready to change your plans.

Babies also grow and develop at different speeds. Some are quick at movement play, but take a while longer to respond to music or sounds. Each baby has her own speed. Don't be worried if she seems to be slow or fast in certain areas. Let her grow at her own rate.

Think About Safety

Remember, babies cannot decide what is safe to play with and what is not. Everything they grab, they put in their mouths. As they get older, they also put things in their noses and ears. It's their way of exploring their world. It's your job to keep unsafe toys and objects away from the baby. You have to make sure the play area is safe as well.

Look carefully at the size of the object you give your baby to play with. Could he swallow it? If so, don't let him play with it. Does it have small parts that could come off and be swallowed? For example, some stuffed animals have little plastic eyes glued on. Your baby could pull off those eyes and push them up his nose or swallow them.

Check to see if toys have sharp or pointed edges. You don't want your baby to jab himself. Be careful with string, cords, or anything else your baby could wrap around his neck. Again, don't let your baby play with anything that isn't safe.

When you're playing the games in this book, stay with your baby. All the games require you to play right there with your baby. This is especially true of bath play. **Never, ever leave your baby alone in or with water. Don't leave for even a minute!**

When you feel sure that your baby is safe, you and he can have a lot more fun together.

Newborns

A newborn's job is to get used to her new world. She spends most of her time sleeping, being active (waving arms and legs around), crying, or watching quietly. The best time to play with your baby is when she is quiet and alert. This usually happens after you have fed her, or after she has been asleep, but is now awake and alert.

When she is quiet and alert, a newborn will pay attention to you for about 4 to 10 seconds at a time. Her attention span will get longer as she gets older. Right now, having her attention for a few seconds is good.

A baby first gets control of her head and neck muscles. Control of her arms, hands, middle body, legs, and feet comes after that.

Simple Faces

Babies like to see simple pictures of people's faces. They usually like pictures of "Mommy" best. Their favorite part of the picture is the eyes.

You will need:
    8½ x 11-inch piece of cardboard
    Drawing paper
    Large, black felt pen
    Glue
    Clear contact paper
    Tape

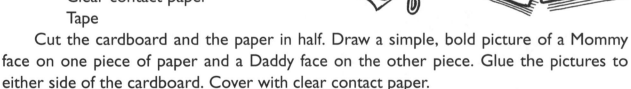

Cut the cardboard and the paper in half. Draw a simple, bold picture of a Mommy face on one piece of paper and a Daddy face on the other piece. Glue the pictures to either side of the cardboard. Cover with clear contact paper.

Tape the picture to the inside of baby's crib for her to look at. Make sure you place the picture down low on the inside of the crib. If she turns her head to the side, she should be able to see the picture. It should be no more than 12 inches away.

Change to the other side after one week. Babies like simple patterns too—like bull's eyes and checkerboards. You can also tape these designs inside the crib.

Movement Play

Gently touching and moving your baby's arms and legs helps her to learn about her own body. She can get to know her arms, legs, hands, and feet. She can also learn that she has two sides to her body.

Lay baby on her back. Gently touch her palms together over the middle of her body. Bring her toes up to touch her nose. Carefully stretch her arms above her head.

Bend her legs at the knee, one after the other, as if she were riding a bicycle.

Talk about each body part as you move it. For example, say, *"These are your toes. Now they're going to touch your nose."*

Kiss and blow on the baby's tummy and hands. Stick out your tongue and wiggle it left to right. Some babies will stick out their tongues back at you.

I can do that, too, Mommy, see.

Rattle Play

 Playing with rattles, or other noisemakers, helps your baby learn to move her head back and forth. She will follow the rattle with her eyes. The crib or the changing table is a good place for this game.

You will need: small rattle

Lay baby on her back. Hold the rattle about a foot away from her face. Shake it gently to get her attention.

Slowly, move the rattle to the left, and then to the right. Watch your baby follow the rattle with her eyes, and then move her head.

Age-1 Month

Your baby will still want to look to the side for a while. It is still important to place things for him to look at on the inside right or left of his crib. He can see clearly only about 12 inches in front of him. Eight inches is his favorite distance right now. That's about how far he has to look to see your face when you are feeding him. He is very interested in your face.

He likes you to cuddle and hold him. He likes soothing sounds—like your voice, or maybe a wind chime. All sorts of normal household sounds are new and interesting to him—like the telephone or family conversations.

The world is still brand new. He is learning every day!

Colored Light Play

Babies will turn their heads and look at bright lights. They also like colored lights. Here are simple ways to show them color and to make baby's room more interesting.

You will need:
> Large, empty jars with lids
> > (pickle jars work well)
>
> Food coloring
> Water
> or,
> Flashlight
> Colored tissue paper or cellophane
> Tape

Fill the jars with water. Put a few drops of different food coloring in each jar. Replace lid tightly and shake. Put the jars in baby's windowsill. When the sunlight shines through the jars, it will create colored light for baby to look at.

Another way to do this is to tape colored tissue paper to a flashlight. Turn out the lights in baby's room. Shine the flashlight right and left over baby's crib. Watch him follow the light with his eyes and head.

Language Play

A baby's first, favorite noise is your natural voice. It comforts him. After all, he listened to your muffled voice for a long time before he was born! He will like to hear you talk, sing, or hum. He will react to high sounds first.

You may feel funny talking to your baby as if he can understand you, but it's a good habit. Right now, the sound of your voice comforts him. Later, he will understand more and more of what you are saying.

When you are doing something with or near your baby, talk to him about what you are doing. For example, say, *"We're going to change your diaper now. This is the clean diaper. This is the washcloth. Now we're taking off your old diaper."*

Tell your baby ahead of time what is going to happen each day. For example, say, *"First we'll put on your coat, and then we'll go outside for a ride in the stroller." "You're going to eat dinner, and then it will be time for bed."*

You can also sing, hum, or say rhymes and poetry to your baby. Mother Goose rhymes are always popular. You can get books of children's poetry from the library. Some well-known songs you might like to try are:

Twinkle, Twinkle, Little Star
Hush, Little Baby, Don't You Cry
Rock-a-Bye Baby
Jingle Bells
I'm a Little Teapot
This Old Man
Three Little Monkeys

Making a Mobile

Mobiles are fun for your baby to look at. They help him to practice focusing his eyes. They are easy to make. Remember that your baby only sees clearly within 12 or so inches of his face.

You will need:
>Ceiling hook (like those used to hang plants)
>Coat hanger
>String or yarn
>Variety of lightweight objects to hang

Put up a ceiling hook over your baby's crib. Tug on it to make sure it is secure. Place it so that the mobile will hang to the side of your baby's face. Curve the hook of the coat hanger so that it makes a closed circle. You don't want the mobile to fall down on your baby.

String or hang three or four different objects on the wide part of the hanger. Use:
>Juice lids
>Brightly colored mittens
>Yarn balls
>Small stuffed animals

Christmas ornaments (non-breakable)
Ball of tin foil
Wooden spoons
Measuring spoons
"God's Eyes" made of brightly
    colored yarn
Scarves
Pictures of black & white bull's eyes
    or checkerboards

You can use many objects for a mobile. This list is just a start. Make sure that the objects you hang have interesting *bottoms* to look at. The bottom of the object is what your baby will see.

String up the mobile so it hangs about eight inches from your baby's face. Change the objects every few days.

Check your mobile for safety. Don't choose objects that are heavy or have sharp or pointed edges. Don't choose objects smaller than 1 x 2 inches.

When your baby gets old enough to bat at the mobile, you can move it closer. You'll want to change the objects to be safe enough to touch.

Age-2 Months

At two months your baby stays awake more often. Her job is still to try to make sense of her world. She sees many colors, hears many sounds, and touches new things everyday. She starts to learn what is part of her body and what belongs to the rest of the world. She starts to watch her hands.

Her favorite way to explore is still to look at things. She will start to play with her hands. She reaches for and bats at things. She smiles. Sometimes she will cuddle with her blanket or stuffed animal.

Smile Play

A smile is fun for everyone. Your baby's first smile will probably be in response to seeing your face. She recognizes you as someone who loves her and takes care of her. There are lots of ways to coax a smile!

Talk or sing to your baby. She loves to hear your voice. Often, all she needs to hear is you talking.

Smile *at* her. Babies love faces. She likes your face best of all. Put your face near hers. Kiss and blow on her fingertips.

Look in the mirror with baby. Say, "*I see the baby! I see the mommy/daddy!*"

Baby Airplane

Moving around is fun for your baby. It helps her learn about her body and her world. This game is fun for parents too.

Pick baby up and hold her firmly around her chest. Lift her up above your head. Say, *"Baby goes up!"*

Lower her down. Say, *"Baby goes down!"* Hold her away from you. Say, *"Baby goes backward!"*

Pull her back toward you. Say, *"Baby goes forward!"* Hold her out from you and turn around. Say, *"Baby goes around!"*

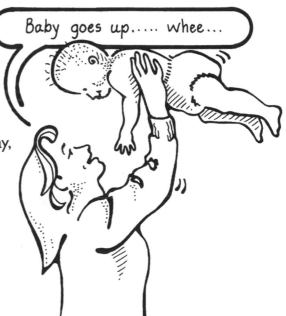

Baby goes up..... whee...

Sound Play

Babies like different kinds of sounds. They learn about their world by listening to the different sounds around them: voices, music, water running, telephones ringing, and much more. You can make different kinds of music and sounds for your baby to listen to. Watch her face to see which sounds she likes.

You will need:

    Music player
    Children's tapes or music
    or, Musical, stuffed animal
    or, Wind chimes
    or, Tape recorder and tape

Hang a wood or wind chime over the baby's crib. Every time you come in, tinkle it gently. Watch your baby turn her head toward the sound.

Or buy a soft, musical stuffed animal for your baby to sleep and cuddle with.

Another idea is to play children's music for your baby.

Some good children's artists are:

Joanie Bartels—*Lullaby Magic, Morningtime Magic,* Discovery Music

Lois Lafond—*Something New (Lullabies),* Lois Lafond & Co.

Marcia Berman—*Marcia Berman Sings Lullabies & Songs You Never Dreamed Were Lullabies,* B&B Records

Raffi—*Singable Songs for the Very Young,* MCA

There are many more. See your local librarian or bookseller for more suggestions.

Tape the sounds your baby makes. Play the tape back to her as often as you like. See if she "talks" back at the tape.

Tape yourself reading children's poetry, rhymes, and stories that you especially like. Your baby will like the sound of your voice and the sound of language. Eventually she will recognize the stories and poems she has been hearing from an early age.

Age-3 Months

Your baby is probably now looking straight ahead. His hands are open. He grabs things with both hands. He can hang onto a rattle. He sleeps less. He cries less. He starts to prefer games he hasn't played before. He has more control over his head and neck muscles.

He now learns to sit with support. His favorite toy is himself. He starts to play with his hands right about this time. He will touch his eyes, nose, and mouth. He might start to smile at you before you smile at him.

Kicking and Batting Play

Your baby has discovered that he can use his feet to kick at things. He can use his hands to bat at things. He likes this. It helps him learn what his body can do.

You will need:
    String
    Half-inch diameter wooden dowel to
        fit across crib and
    (Choose from the following)
    Small stuffed animals
    Empty thread spools
    Rattle
    Bath sponges

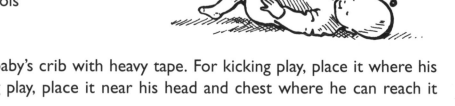

Attach dowel to the baby's crib with heavy tape. For kicking play, place it where his feet can reach. For batting play, place it near his head and chest where he can reach it with his hands.

String the dowel with three or four of the objects listed above. Your baby will soon bat and kick at the objects. Change the objects as he gets bored with them.

It is also fun to hang a small stuffed animal from the ceiling with elastic. Let your baby bat at the toy.

Place an air-filled punching toy at your baby's feet for him to kick. It will pop back up each time he hits it.

Safety note: Make sure the objects you use do not have sharp or pointed edges that could hurt your baby. Also take care that there are no long, trailing ends of elastic or string that your baby could wrap around his neck.

Nose Play

Offering baby a smell of something he likes can be fun. It teaches him about different strong smells. If he doesn't like something, don't offer it again. Stick to the smells he likes.

You will need:

      Vanilla bottle
      Cinnamon & sugar mixture
      Dill pickle
      Garlic powder
      Mild perfume

Hold the vanilla bottle under his nose. Move it back and forth. Watch your baby's face. Does he like the smell? If so, say, *"You like to smell vanilla."* If not, say, *"You don't like to smell vanilla"* and put it away.

Repeat with the other materials.

Bath Play

Bath time offers many different feelings for your baby. He can feel the difference between wet and dry, cold and warm, and slippery-soap and towel-dry. He can hear the splashing of the water and the noise of the drain. Water is fun to look at and touch. It moves and catches the light.

Be gentle with him and go slowly. If he seems unsure or afraid of anything, stop or slow down.

Hold your baby in an upright position in the bath. Be careful, wet babies are slippery!

Allow him to kick and splash as much as he likes. Gently splash him back on his body. Trickle water on him. Move him slowly through the water.

Safety note: running the cold water and then the warm water helps to keep the bottom of the tub from getting too hot.

Test the water with your elbow before you put him in. Remember, babies like

water cooler than adults. Limit bath time so that he doesn't get chilled.

Remember never to leave him alone in or by the tub of water. Not even for a minute!

Age-4 Months

Baby is beginning to know who she is. You have helped her grow from a helpless newborn into an active baby who is ready to learn more about the world. She flings her arms out. She responds to your voice with gurgling. She laughs, kicks, grabs things and lets them go. She can see farther away. She sleeps and stays awake for longer stretches. She starts to reach for things.

It is now time to put away any fragile mobiles and batting toys. She is able to touch, taste, and hold whatever takes her fancy. Anything she can touch should be safe enough to go into her mouth and not be swallowed.

Nursery Rhymes and Chants

The nonsense words in nursery rhymes are fun for babies. The rhymes and rhythms will help her to learn to listen. She will like to hear these chants and rhymes over and over again. Chant or sing these rhymes.

Pease, Porridge Hot
Pease, porridge hot,
Pease, porridge cold,
Pease, porridge in the pot,
Nine days old!

Eeeney, Meeney, Miney, Mo
Eeeney, meeney, miney, mo,
Catch a finger or a toe,
If it hollers, let it go,
Eeeney, meeney, miney, mo.

Hey, Diddle, Diddle
Hey, diddle, diddle,
The cat and the fiddle,
The cow jumped over the moon.
The little dog laughed to see such a sight,
And the dish ran away with the spoon.

Hickory, Dickory, Dock
Hickory, dickory, dock,
The mouse ran up the clock.
The clock struck one,
The mouse ran down,
Hickory, dickory, dock.

Try some of these well-known chants with common toe or finger plays:

This Little Piggy Went to Market

This little piggy went to market,
This little piggy stayed home.
This little piggy had roast beef,
This little piggy had none.
And this little piggy cried wee, wee, wee,
all the way home.

Here's the Church

Here's the church,
Here's the steeple,
Open the doors,
And see all the people!

HERE'S THE CHURCH,

HERE'S THE STEEPLE

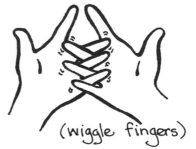

OPEN THE DOORS,
AND SEE ALL THE PEOPLE!

(wiggle fingers)

Peek-a-Boo

Games are more fun for your baby when you play too. Because your baby is interested in you, she will be interested in games you play with her. She still likes faces. Peek-a-boo is a good "face" game. She hasn't learned yet that people and things she can't see still exist. This game will help her start to learn this. She'll like this game for a long time.

You will need:

     Blanket (optional)

     Puppet or stuffed animal (optional)

First, smile at your baby. Put your hands over your eyes, then over your baby's eyes. Say, *"Peek-a-boo!"*

Put a baby blanket over *your head*. Lift it up and say, *"Peek-a-boo!"*

Bring out a puppet. Hold the puppet in front of your baby and say, *"Peek-a-boo!"* Put it behind your back for a moment. Then bring it out again and say, *"Peek-a-boo!"* If she likes it, she may smile.

Touchy-Feely Toys

Your baby is now exploring with her hands. You can let her touch many different things. This is how she learns where her body stops and where other things begin. This game also helps baby begin to learn about left and right.

You will need:

      Plastic "squeak" toys
      Cold, smooth baking pans (like muffin tins)
      Small bean bags (sewn tightly)
      Wooden or plastic napkin rings
      Small stuffed animals
      Measuring spoons
      Cloth books
      Rubber or plastic balls (size of tennis ball)

Prop your baby up into a sitting position. Set out three "toys" in front of her.

Starting with the toy on the left, move it close to her. See if she will reach out and grasp it. Give her time to touch and mouth the toy. Put it back in the row.

Do the same thing with the other toys. Work left to right. You can change the toys and play the game again later.

Age-5 Months

Baby's hands are busy most of the time. He can pass things from one hand to another. Many babies look carefully at the things they scoop up. He can probably roll over by now. He likes to push with his feet.

His babbling is more meaningful. You can tell if he means, "Look at me," "Pick me up," or "I don't like it." He is likely to cry angrily when he doesn't get what he wants. He can tell the difference between strangers and people he knows. He definitely wants his parents when he is scared or unhappy.

Drop & Pick Up

This game helps baby learn to move, watch, and listen. Learning how one action makes something happen (cause and effect) is important for babies. It helps them learn about the rules of the natural world.

You will need:

An object to drop—it could be:
Colorful plastic ring
Measuring spoons
Silver spoon
Clothespin
Rattle

Sit baby on the floor. Show him a spoon. Let him look at, feel, and taste it.

Hold it slightly higher than his face. Drop it. Encourage him to watch and listen for the sound it makes when it hits the ground. Say, *"Look at the spoon go down!"*

Drop the spoon several times, each time saying, *"Down!"*

Let your baby hold the spoon again. Does he try to drop or throw it? Pick up the spoon and give it back to baby to drop. Do this until he gets tired of the game.

You can repeat the game at other times with other objects.

Baby Be Nimble Game

Babies like to bounce around with their parents. They enjoy rhymes and games that have a "surprise ending." When you play this game you will help him build his memory.

Bounce the baby on your knee. Make up a rhyme, or use the following:

> *Baby be nimble,*
> *Baby be quick,*
> *Baby jump over the candlestick!*

Move baby to the other knee when you chant the last line. Your baby will learn to expect this surprise ending. He may start to smile or laugh before you switch knees. This shows how his memory is growing.

Ring Pull

This game will help your baby learn to pull himself forward. It also allows him to solve a problem (get from one spot to another) all by himself.

You will need:

      Large plastic ring

      Scarf

Tie one end of the scarf to the ring. Tie the other scarf end tightly to the head of the baby's crib. Set the baby near the ring. Watch him learn to grasp the ring and pull himself forward. **Safety note: Make sure the scarf is not too long. You don't want the baby to wrap it around his neck.**

Stay with your baby while he plays with the ring pull. Remove the toy from the crib when he is tired of it.

Age-6 Months

Some babies are now sitting by themselves. Your baby may be scooting or creeping on her tummy. She will hold a toy in each hand. She is getting better at using her thumb when she picks up things. Her eyesight is getting better and better. She may even try to pick up crumbs on the floor. She can tell the difference between a happy and a sad face. She likes sounds of all kinds—especially toys that make sounds.

She might start to be shy, or even scared, with people other than her parents. This usually means that she loves you best and is a little afraid you might leave if a new person comes in. Once she's used to the new person being there, she will relax.

Don't Stop Game

At this age babies start to learn that people, not objects, make things happen. It is fun to see if your baby will try to get you to keep playing this game.

Hold baby's arms with your hands and put her on your foot. Bounce the baby gently. Sing, or chant rhymes.

Stop moving and talking all at once. Try to keep your face still. What does your baby do to get you to play again? She may bounce, babble, or wave her arms.

Reward her efforts. Start playing again.

Drum Play

Drums are a fun way to make noise. Your baby can learn about how to make a sound when she hits the drum with her hands or a spoon.

You will need:

Oatmeal box (round)
Tape or glue
Wooden spoon

Tape or glue the lid back onto an empty oatmeal box. It will make a good drum. Show your baby how to pound on it. Try showing her a "1, 2" rhythm.

To change things a bit, let her use different kinds of spoons to hit the drum. Say, "Hmmm. *That silver spoon makes a different sound, doesn't it?*"

Hide the Toy Game

This game shows you how to half-hide a toy for your baby to find. Your baby is slowly learning that when she can't see something, it still exists. This game will help her problem solve while she learns.

You will need:

>Baby's favorite toy, such as a rattle or stuffed animal
>Blanket

Hide half of the toy under baby's blanket. Make sure a little bit of the toy shows. Let the baby see the toy. She will learn to pull the blanket off and "discover" the toy. Repeat this game as long as your baby wants to play it.

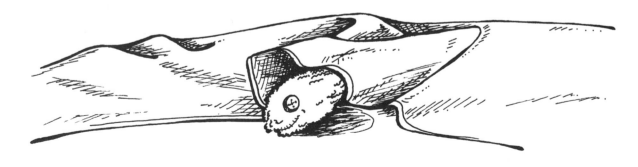

Age-7 Months

Your baby can probably sit up by himself at seven months. He has been able to roll over for a little while now. He'll pick up something, play with it, and then move on to another toy. If you interrupt him, he'll stop for a moment, and then go back to his play. This shows his growing memory and ability to think.

He's been getting teeth. Some babies begin to crawl now. He can use his thumb and fingers better. He's interested in pictures and patterns, shapes and sizes. He knows now that a toy exists when he can't see it. Watch him look for a toy after he drops it.

He's been babbling for some time, but now he starts to know his own name.

Bang Bang Game

Your baby likes to explore different shapes and sizes. You can give him toys that will help him learn about "front and back" and "top and bottom."

You will need:

> Two blocks
> Two pie tins
> Two toy balls
> Two board books

Sit your baby on the floor. Show him two blocks. Let him look at and explore them. Show him how to bang the blocks together. Say, *"Bang, bang!"*

Repeat the game with the pie tins and board books. Watch how he looks at and feels the different shapes.

Repeat the activity with the two balls. Does he look for corners on the balls? Look for the top? Look for the bottom, front, or back?

Books, Books, Books

Even very young babies can learn to love books. If he learns that books mean fun time with you, he will look forward to storytime. Reading aloud to him helps him learn to listen for rhythm and rhyme, and he will like looking at the pictures.

You will need:

Board books or cloth books (from library or bookstore)
For suggested titles, see pages 113-115.

Pick a time when your baby is likely to pay attention. Some babies like to sit so that they can see *your* face as you read.

Read the book together. Let him turn the pages as you read. He may like to turn pages more than listen to the story or look at pictures. That's okay. Turning pages is part of the fun of books.

Name the objects in the pictures. Say, *"Where is the baby?"* or, *"I see the teddy bear!"*

Read the book as many times in a row as baby likes. He will love reading the same thing again and again.

Block Play

With your help, your baby can start to learn how to stack things. Blocks are a fun way to start. His favorite part will be knocking a simple block tower down. This game helps him practice seeing something and then touching it. It will help him understand "down" better. And it encourages him to copy you.

You will need:

Blocks or spools

Show baby how to stack two or three blocks on top of one another. Don't use more than three. Help him if he needs it. Say, *"Good job! Look at that block tower you built!"*

Then show him how to knock the blocks down. Say, *"Down!"* Clap and smile when he knocks the blocks down. Repeat game as long as baby likes.

Age-8 Months

Your baby is creeping and soon will be crawling around your house. Some babies learn to creep up stairs at this age. She explores with her hands, eyes, ears, mouth, and nose. Nearly everything interests her.

She grows even more shy around new people or places. This is because her memory is growing. She can now tell what is new from what she already knows. If the situation or person is new, she can't tell what will happen. This can be scary, and so she acts shy or even upset. She likes to keep track of you. She is starting to learn that even though you go away (or out of the room), you come back.

She likes to solve problems. When she puts the plastic keys into a bucket, she wonders, will they still be there when the bucket is dumped upside down? If she hears a sound, she looks to see where it came from. This is a fun age for games.

Hat and Mirror Game

By playing this game you will help your baby learn where her head is. Using the mirror helps her see how her hands work to do what she wants.

You will need:

> Two or three hats (small, if possible)
> Light plastic bowl
> Mirror

Sit down with your baby in front of a wall or door mirror. Put a hat on her head. Say, *"The hat is on baby's head!"* Point to her head in the mirror. Let her take the hat off and put it back on. Watch her try to find her head. Repeat with the other hat and the bowl.

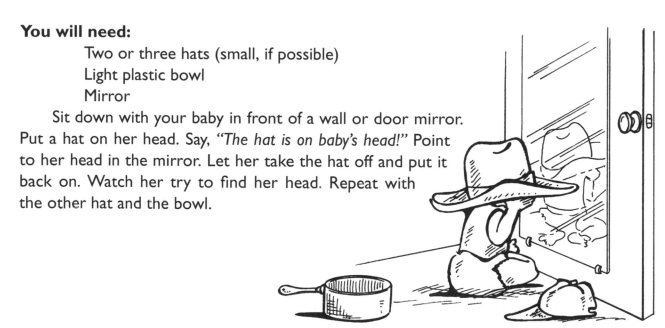

Make That Sound!

This game will help your baby connect the noises she hears with the things that make them. It will also prompt her to mimic you with sounds.

Each day, find something around the house you can imitate the sound of. Some possibilities are:

Ticking clock
Washing machine
Running water
Vacuum cleaner
Cat meowing
Doorbell

Say, *"Baby, listen!"* Mimic the sound. Touch the object that makes the sound. Make the sound again. Try to pick sounds that are not frightening. Repeat with other objects.

Pot Puzzle

Pots and pans can be fun puzzles. As your baby learns to put a lid on a pot, she is learning how shapes fit together.

You will need:
>   Small pot with lid
>   Medium-sized pot with lid
>   Small toy

Show your baby how to put a lid on the small pot. Help her learn how to do it herself. After she becomes good at it, give her the medium-sized pot and lid. Watch her try to figure out which lid goes with which pot. Let her bang the lids together.

For fun, hide a small toy in one of the pots. Watch her surprise when she finds it.

Age-9 Months

This is an age at which babies differ a lot. Some babies are crawling all over the place. Some babies sit happily, or have just learned to scoot along on their bottoms. Some babies are learning about small objects like spoons. Other babies are now learning to let go when they hand you a toy.

All babies grow at different rates. They learn quickly, and then slow down. They need time to get used to a new skill. Your baby probably opens cupboards, takes out things, and plays with them. He understands some words and phrases. He might say "bye bye" or "mama," or "dada" by now.

Since he gets into just about everything, it's a good idea to have a place in every room your baby goes into that has toys just for him.

Drop and Dump Game

This is a kind of hide-and-seek game for babies. Putting toys in containers and then dumping them out helps baby learn that the toys still exist even when they are out of sight. This game is a fun one because baby can do it all by himself.

You will need:

     Empty, open oatmeal container
     A few differently shaped and colored blocks or
     other small toys

Put the blocks or toys in the oatmeal container. Show your baby the oatmeal box, or wait for him to find it.

Watch how he finds the toys inside and dumps them out. Does he hold and look at them and then put one or two back in the box? Let him drop the toys in and dump them out as long as he likes. He will probably like dumping the toys out best.

Touch-Me Board

This toy is easy to make and fun for your baby to play with. It helps him learn about colors, shapes, and textures.

You will need:

Scraps of brightly colored fabric of different textures. Some good scraps are:

Velvet or velveteen
Dotted swiss
Brocade
Carpet scraps
Satin
Wool
Corduroy
Terry cloth
Fake fur
Quilted fabric
Light cardboard or poster board
Glue

Cut out squares of material into 5 x 5-inch pieces. Glue them onto the cardboard in rows of three or four.

Let your baby feel each square, one at a time. Talk about what he feels. Say, *"Satin feels smooth. This one feels bumpy. Corduroy feels rough."* Watch and see which ones he likes to feel the most.

Eensy Weensy Spider

This is an old song that babies love. It makes diaper-changing time more fun for everyone, and helps baby learn to listen.

Sing:

*The eensy-weensy spider
Climbed up the water spout.
Down came the rain
And washed the spider out.
Out came the sun,
And dried up all the rain.
The eensy-weensy spider
Climbed up the spout again.*

As you sing, pretend your fingers are the spider and walk up and down your baby's leg. You can add other hand gestures of your own. Sing the song a few times.

Try stopping suddenly in the middle of the song. If your baby gestures or babbles, say, *"Oh, you want more."* Then start singing again.

Age-10 Months

Many babies pull themselves up to stand by this age. Your baby can stack one block on top of another. She is starting to tell the difference between big and small. A big cat might scare her, whereas she might be happy to touch a small kitten.

She knows how many things should look. For example, if you hand her a bowl upside down, she'll turn it over. She likes to drop toys and fill up containers.

She knows the voices of her parents and brothers and sisters. She tries to copy sounds you make. She is starting to be braver about being away from you. However, most babies still want you very near them in a new place. Many babies also are sad to say goodnight to their parents and go to sleep.

Tube Games

Cardboard tubes are fun to play with. You can give your baby all sorts of learning experiences with sound, sight, and touch.

You will need:

Cardboard tube from a roll of paper towels
Colorful scarves

Sit down with your baby. Talk to her through the tube. Disguise or vary your voice. Watch how you catch her attention.

Make silly sounds. Blow through the tube. Give the tube to her. See if she tries to talk or blow back at you.

Tie a few scarves together. Let your baby pull them through the tube. Does she try to stuff them back into the tube?

Safety note: Do not let your baby play with the scarves alone. Never leave a baby alone to play with something that she could wrap around her neck.

Muffin Tin Play

This game is the very start of learning to count. Your baby will enjoy putting objects into the muffin tin holes.

You will need:

      Six-cup muffin tin

      Six tennis balls, or small bean bags

Give your baby a muffin tin. Show her how to place a ball into each hole. Take turns putting the balls in and taking them out.

Let her dump them all out and start over.

Pulling and Poking Play

Your baby is already good at grabbing what she wants. This game will help her practice letting go. She is also starting to poke at things. This game will let her do that too.

You will need:

    Small block with round hole in it
    or, Plastic key ring
    or, Toilet paper tube cut in half
    or, Wooden napkin ring
    Piece of elastic 12 to 15 inches long

Tie one end of the elastic to the block or toy. Tie the other end to a piece of furniture (or somewhere the baby can easily reach) so that it hangs freely.

Show her how to pull the toy and let it bounce back several times. Does she copy you? She might also explore the object and poke her finger into it.

For a change, tie the toy to baby's high chair. Put her in the chair and see if she pulls the toy up to play with it.

Safety note: Do not leave your baby alone when she's playing this game. She could choke if she wraps the elastic around her neck.

Age-11 Months

Most babies are crawling at this age. Some are walking and others are pulling themselves up to stand. Most can walk holding onto a parent's hands. Your baby's language skills are growing. He understands many words you use. He uses some sounds of his own. Some babies say a word or two by this time. He pays more attention to how things feel—like gooey or sticky. He may dislike some of these feelings.

Your baby recognizes family and friends. Does he offer them toys when they come in? This is his way of saying hello. He likes to be where the action is. He is also developing a sense of humor. He might laugh if you do the opposite of what he expects. For example, pretend to drink out of his bottle, or put on his sock.

Copy Cat Game

This game helps your baby start learning about following directions. It also helps him learn to listen.

You will need:
> Teddy bear
> Ball
> Hat

Sit down with your baby. Place the teddy bear, ball, and hat in front of him, left to right.

Pick up the bear. Hug it. Say, *"Mommy hugs the teddy bear."* Tell your baby to hug the teddy bear. If he does it, clap and smile. Say, *"Baby hugs the bear!"* If he doesn't, hug the bear again. Encourage him to copy you. Continue this until he loses interest.

Pick up the ball. Roll it to your baby. Say, *"Mommy rolls the ball."* Show your baby how to roll it back to you. Say, *"Baby rolls the ball."* Continue until he loses interest.

Pick up the hat. Put it on your head. Say, *"Mommy puts the hat on her head."* Show your baby how to put it on his head. Say, *"Baby puts the hat on his head!"*

Remember to smile and clap every time your baby copies you. He will learn faster if you praise him. He likes to play these games over and over.

Feeling Faces

Everyone has feelings. Your baby has been watching you feel happy, sad, frustrated, or proud since he was born. You can start to give him words for simple feelings. And you can help him learn that people's faces show what they feel.

You will need:
>   Paper
>   Felt marker
>   Glue
>   Cardboard or poster board

Draw simple faces showing the feelings: happy, sad, surprised, excited, or mad.

Glue the pictures onto a large piece of cardboard. Set it up where the baby can see it. Say, *"Baby, let's make a happy face."* Point to the happy face on the board. Make your face into a happy face. Prompt him to look at you and at the picture.

Repeat with the other pictures. See if your baby will copy you.

Touching and Feeling Play

Your baby learns a lot about the world through his sense of touch. The more experiences you provide, the more he will learn.

You will need:
>Uncooked oatmeal
>Stickers, or scotch tape
>Powder
>Glass of crushed ice

Let your baby play with a small amount of uncooked oatmeal in a bowl or on a tray. Watch him run his hands through it. Don't let him eat too much of it.

Give your baby a sticker, or a piece of tape to play with while you change his diaper. Say, *"It's sticky, isn't it?"* Let him play with it until he loses interest.

Put some powder on the floor. Help your baby walk through it barefoot. Talk about it. Say, *"Powder feels smooth."*

Let your baby hold and munch on crushed ice. Say, "Ice is cold." **Safety note: Make sure the ice is too small to choke on.**

Put your baby's hands under the faucet. Run warm water. Say, *"This water is warm."*

Age-12 Months

Some babies are walking at this age. Some are crawling and some are climbing. All of them are getting around the house happily. Your baby is actively exploring her world with her eyes, hands, and legs. She is becoming more independent in her play every day.

She is learning how to tease. You might see her hold out a toy to someone and then pull it back, smiling. She copies your sounds and what you do. She might use one-word sentences. She understands your words much more than you think.

Picture Blocks

Your baby knows family member's faces and their names too. This is a fun game for your baby to show off this skill.

You will need:
> Two empty milk cartons
> Newspaper
> Contact paper
> Glue
> Photos of family and friends

Wash out two milk cartons. Cut them in half, 5 inches or so from the bottom. Throw away the halves with the spout. Stuff one carton half with newspaper. Push the two halves together to form a cube. Cover the block with contact paper.

Glue pictures of different family members onto each side. Show your baby all the pictures. Ask her to point out Mommy, Daddy, brother, Grandma, etc.

For fun, point to Daddy and say, *"Is this Grandma?"* Your baby will enjoy the joke.

Nesting Play

Your baby is very interested in how some objects fit inside one another. She will try to push together objects that don't fit. Many household objects are perfect for this game.

You will need:

> Measuring spoons on a ring
> or, Measuring cups that nest
> > inside of one another
>
> or, Pots and pans that nest
> > inside of one another
>
> or, Baskets that nest inside of one another

Show your baby how these objects fit inside each other. At first, just use one set of objects at a time. Let her take them apart and fit them together. Watch her try all sorts of combinations.

As your baby gets good at this, give her two sets of objects. Watch how she puts cups in the baskets, or baskets in the pots.

Silly Pull Toy

You don't have to buy expensive toys for your baby to learn. As you have already seen, she likes to play with many ordinary objects around the house. This toy helps your baby practice her pulling skills. You can make it with items you don't need anymore.

You will need:
>String, cord, or sturdy yarn
>Curlers
>Empty thread spools
>Odd blocks, with a hole drilled in the center
>Large beads
>Keys
>Bells
>Empty cans with top and bottom cut out (make sure edges are not sharp)

String together the items you have gathered. Make sure some of those items make interesting noises. Leave enough string for her to pull the toy with.

Show your baby how to pull her new toy along the floor.

Safety note: Remember to watch your baby when she plays with string—you don't want her to wrap it around her neck.

Growing from Babies to Toddlers

As your baby grows and passes that one-year-old mark, she becomes a toddler. Children ages 12 months through two years are toddlers. The following list will show what young toddlers, ages 12 months to 18 months, are like.

A young toddler . . .
Pays attention for only a short time.
Shows wants without crying.
Walks.
Knows some body parts.
Responds to spoken requests.
Builds a tower of two blocks.
Scribbles on her own.

Crawls down stairs backwards.
Starts to play by herself.
Moves toys and objects around.
Solves simple problems.
May strongly prefer mother.
Drinks well from a cup.
Uses simple words, names.

No two toddlers are alike. Some toddlers will do these things at 12 months and others will do them at 18 months. Still others will do them a little after 18 months. All of them are normal.

The following pages have more games and fun ways to play with your toddler. She will still like many of the games you played with her as a baby. But now she is ready for more.

Age 12-15 Months

Mirror Play

This is a fun game for a toddler who is fussy or bored. He will have fun watching and copying you.

You will need:

A mirror

Hold your toddler up to a mirror. Say, "See the baby? Let's kiss him. Let's wave to him. Where are his toes? Where is his nose?" See if your child will do what you do.

Kitchen Cupboard Play

Your toddler can have fun exploring and playing while you are fixing meals.

You will need:

A low, kitchen cupboard or drawer that your toddler can have for his own
Various kitchen dishes and utensils

Fill the cupboard with safe and fun
kitchen utensils and dishes.
Some ideas are:

Measuring spoons
Plastic plates and cup
Wooden spoons
Different-sized pots and
pans with lids

From time to time, change the things in the cupboard and surprise him. Help him put the things back in the drawer when he finishes playing. Always do this with him and make it fun. (He's not ready to be responsible for picking up after himself.)

Chase & Catch

You are your toddler's favorite toy. This game is a fun way to be active and enjoy each other.

Get down on your hands and knees and crawl after your toddler. Say, *"I'm going to catch you!"* Then give her a big hug. Invite her to chase you. Say, *"Can you catch me?"* and crawl ahead. Let her catch you and hug her again.

Rocks & Water

This activity helps toddlers notice the colors and feel of the rocks.

You will need:
>   Small bucket
>   Variety of rocks
>   Bowl & water

Go outside and collect some different-sized rocks. Choose rocks that she can't swallow. Put them in a bucket. Put some water in a bowl. Show your child how to wash each rock. Talk about how each one looks different. Say, *"Look, this rock got dark when we washed it! This rock looks pink. That one looks black."* **Safety note: Stay with your toddler when she is around water. She can drown in as little as one inch of water in a bucket if she falls in.** Make sure she doesn't throw the rocks either.

What Does the Animal Say?

Toddlers enjoy recognizing animals and making their sounds. Your toddler will enjoy playing this game over and over again.

You will need:
>   Old magazines

Collect pictures of animals out of magazines or newspapers. Some good ones are: dog, cat, cow, horse, sheep, duck. Point to each picture and ask your toddler, *"What does this one say? That's right, the cow says MOO."*

Jingle Bell Toddler

Tie one or two bells to your toddler's shoes when it gets close to the winter holidays. Encourage her to dance to music and make the bells ring. Sing *Jingle Bells* with her.

Simple Puzzles

Toddlers are learning about how shapes fit together. You can make simple puzzles out of heavy cardboard.

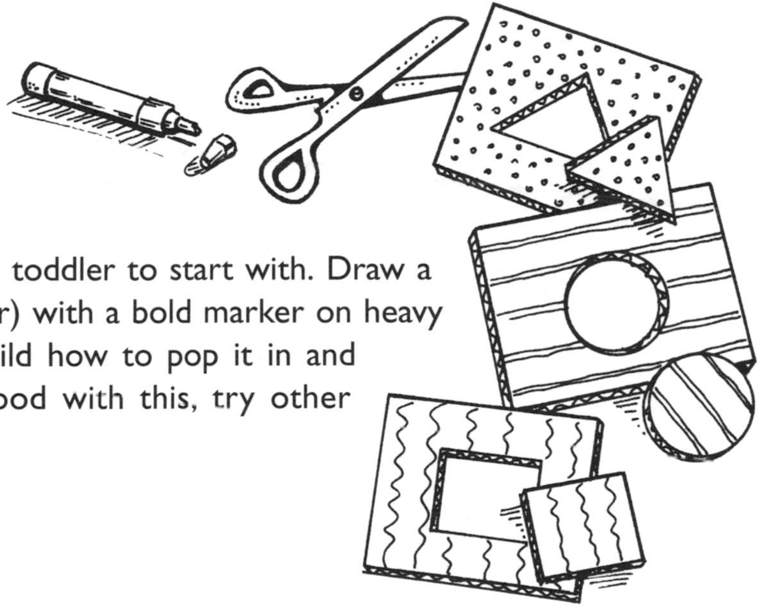

You will need:
- Heavy cardboard
- Scissors
- Bold marker

A circle is the easiest shape for a toddler to start with. Draw a circle (about 3 to 5 inches in diameter) with a bold marker on heavy cardboard. Cut it out. Show your child how to pop it in and out of the cardboard. As he gets good with this, try other shapes.

A Worm Hunt

Worms are fun for toddlers to hold and feel. Go on a walk in your neighborhood or park and look for worms. They like to come out just after it rains. Or bring a spade and dig a little. Have your child touch the worm gently. Talk about how worms get their food from the dirt. Make sure your child is gentle and returns the worm to the dirt.

Hug a Tree

While you are outside, on a walk, or at the park, look at the trees. Talk about how some are very tall and wide, and others are tall and skinny. Touch the bark and name it. Say, *"This bark feels rough"* or *"This bark feels smooth."* Invite your child to give the tree a hug if she wants. Say, *"Good-bye, tree!"*

Where's the Toddler?

This is a fun game to play in the car with your child. If he gets fussy or bored, ask, *"Where's Johnny [his name]?"* Look from side to side. Point out the window, *"Is he there?"* Point somewhere else, *"Is he there?"* Then point to the child, *"There he is!"* Your toddler

will smile and shake his head no and yes when you play this game. Repeat for Mommy, Daddy, and anyone else riding in the car.

This game is also fun to play around the house. Stay in one room so you can be sure your toddler is safe. Pretend to look all around, saying, *"Where's Johnny?"* Then "find" him suddenly and exclaim, *"There you are!"* He will probably laugh at you.

Age 15-18 Months

A Full Purse

Toddlers like to fill things up and carry them around. An old purse is great for this. They like to put things in the purse that are like what you have in your purse or wallet.

You will need:
- Purse
- Comb
- Brush
- Wallet
- Junk mail
- Keys

Give your child the purse and the items to fill it with. Anything that was once yours will be fun for her. Let her fill it up and carry it around. The full purse is a fun toy to take with you in the car and on errands.

Fun with Bubbles

Toddlers like to touch everything when they are exploring. Bubbles are a fun, safe thing to touch and pop.

You will need:
> Bottle of bubbles
> Bunch of straws

Buy a bottle of bubbles or make your own. Add two tablespoons dishwashing liquid to one cup of water. Add a drop of food coloring if you wish. Tape four or five straws together and dip them in the bubbles. Show your toddler how to blow the bubbles through the straw bundle. Have fun chasing and popping the bubbles.

Safety note: Baby should not suck in the bubble soap. Be sure he knows how to blow out before teaching him this game.

Row, Row, Row Your Boat!

Sit on the floor with your legs straight and apart, facing your toddler. Stretch your arms out and hold her hands. Sing this old nursery song:

Row, row, row your boat,
Gently down the stream.
Merrily, merrily, merrily, merrily,
Life is but a dream.

As you sing, lean back and forth and gently pull your toddler to and fro. Your toddler will like the singing and the movement. She will learn to sing the song, too.

Jumping Fun

Toddlers love to jump! They are active and on-the-move. If you're tired of him jumping on the bed, offer these other jumping places: a pile of leaves or a small mud puddle. He will enjoy jumping from a 2 x 6-inch wooden balance beam placed 6 inches off the floor or ground, or over a pile of dirt. Couch cushions or pillows, or a pile of pillows, are also safe and fun to jump on. A broom to jump *over* is also fun.

Making Decisions

All toddlers need practice making decisions. Offer your toddler choices whenever you can. Some common choices might be:

"Would you like to sit in the big chair or the little chair?"
"Would you like a whole cookie or a half cookie?"
"Which doll would you like to play with?"
"Do you want to wear your red or blue shirt today?"

This game helps her build social skills. Remember only to offer choices you like. Make sure they are safe.

Would you like to play this game or that game?

Toys in Jars

Your toddler will like solving the problem in this game.

You will need:
> Small, plastic jar (like a peanut butter jar) with lid
> Small stuffed animal or toy to fit in jar

Make sure the jar is washed well and the lid is small enough to fit in small hands. Put the toy inside and screw the lid back on the jar. Set the jar down in front of your child. See if he figures out how to unscrew the lid and find the toy. He may even put it back in!

Ring-Around-the-Rosy

This is a classic game most toddlers love. You can play it with just two people or you can include a favorite doll or stuffed animal. Chant the words:

Ring around the rosy,
Pockets full of posies,
Ashes, ashes,
We all fall down!

Your toddler will probably want to play this over and over again.

Finger Puppets

This is a fun thing to do on a long car ride, or during a wait at the doctor's office. It will help your child learn to use his imagination.

Draw a face (eyes, nose, and mouth) on two of your fingertips (one finger on each hand). Wiggle your fingers as the puppets "talk" to each other. Draw two faces on your child's fingers. See if he has his two puppets talk to each other.

Playing with "Real" Toys

You can make some adult things you don't need anymore safe and fun for toddlers. Young children love to play with real, old telephones. An old battery-operated radio is fun for toddlers to turn on and off, change the station, and to turn the volume way up and way down. Your toddler will have fun copying the grown-ups with these "real" toys.

Safety note: Make sure you carefully check these items before giving them to your child. The knobs and buttons should be sturdy and well attached. Cut off the electrical cords so that baby can't plug in the toys.

Making Sandwiches

Toddlers like to be independent. Making her own sandwich is a fun thing your toddler can do for herself. She can spread butter, peanut butter, tuna fish, or jam on bread. Give her a blunt, table knife to use, and watch her carefully.

Give the Doll a Bath

Toddlers like to copy their parents. This game gives them a chance to copy bath-time.

You will need:
Doll
Empty plastic tub
Small bar of soap
Washcloth
Towel

Give your child a doll (with clothes on) and the other bath-time items. Say, *"Can you give the doll a bath?"* See if he remembers to take the clothes off. Watch him have fun washing and dressing the baby. Both boys and girls like to play this game.

Shaving Cream Fun

Even toddlers who usually don't like to get their hands messy will like this art activity.

You will need:

      Big, clean table space

      Can of shaving cream

Clear a big space on a table. Spray some shaving cream on the table for your toddler to touch, spread, and finger paint with. Give yourself some, too, and do it with her. Shaving cream smells good and feels good. Watch your child carefully to make sure she doesn't eat the shaving cream or get it in her eyes.

Sticky Picture Fun

Your toddler will like seeing how different things feel. This art activity will let him play with stickiness.

You will need:

> Contact paper
> Muffin tin
> Things to stick:
>> Small pictures cut out of magazines
>> Pieces of colorful ribbon
>> Leaves
>> Feathers

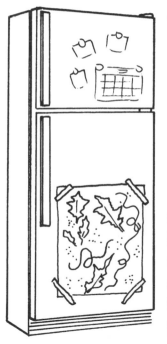

Cut out a large square of contact paper. Tape it to the refrigerator, sticky side out. Put the things to stick in the muffin tin. Show your child how to stick things on the contact paper. Let him decide what will go on the picture. He may only like to touch the stickiness with his fingers. Tell him, *"You're making art."* When he finishes, you can save the picture by covering it with clear contact paper.

Tape-a-Story

Older toddlers love to hear their favorite stories over and over again. This is a fun and different way to read together. It will help your child learn to follow directions.

You will need:

    Storybook

    Tape recorder

Tape yourself reading a favorite storybook to your toddler. Remember to say on the tape things like, *"Turn the page now"* to help her follow along. Give her the book and turn on the tape for her.

Let's Talk About Toys

Young children learn by playing. Many toys help babies and toddlers learn about the world. Some toys turn out to be a waste of money. As one mother said, *"I have this expensive activity gym for my baby, but she likes playing with a two-cent paper bag better!"* You don't have to buy your child lots of expensive toys. She can learn just as well with "toys" you have around the house.

Toys for Babies

Here is a list of things you probably already have that babies like to play with:

    Pie tins
    Tennis balls
    Old purse
    Pots and pans with covers
    Cardboard tubes (from paper towels or toilet paper)
    Shoe boxes
    Wooden & plastic spoons
    Drawers or cupboard doors to open and close
    Colored sponges
    Bells (big enough not to be swallowed)
    Nesting measuring spoons and cups

Toys you can buy (or sometimes make yourself):

    Pail and shovel
    Dolls
    Blocks (wooden)
    Music box

Stuffed animals
Color cone (big-to-small rings on a peg)
Jack-in-the-Box
Plastic shapes (circle, square, triangle) to drop into a box with same shape
holes

Toys for Toddlers

Toddlers are very busy, don't pay attention for very long, and touch everything. As with babies, toys don't need to be fancy or expensive. Many good toddler toys are simple, household items. Toddlers like toys that look real—a bus that looks like a bus, or a doll that looks like a baby. The toy reminds them of the real thing.

Toddler toys you may already have on hand:
Big cardboard box
Soap bubbles and wands
Rocks (medium-sized) to put in and dump out of containers
Plastic dishes
Old telephone
Sand

Safe kitchen utensils & bowls
Dress-up clothes
Water & cups for filling and dumping
Band-Aid™ boxes

Toys you may wish to buy:
Puzzles with 2 to 3 big pieces
Stacking toys
Dolls
Screw toys
Stuffed animals
Rubber or soft balls
Cars, trains, trucks, buses, airplanes
Duplo® bricks (large Legos®)
Blocks

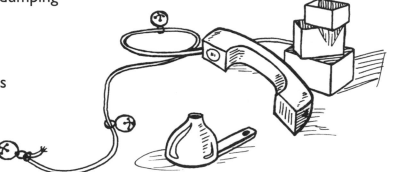

Here are some tips to keep in mind as you look for toys for babies and toddlers:

Make sure the toy is safe. Babies and toddlers shouldn't play with toys that have small pieces or parts that they can swallow. Toys that have long strings that could get wrapped around their necks are dangerous. Toys with sharp edges, that have lead paint

on them, or contain hidden wires are also dangerous.

The toy needs to be fun and not too hard for the child to work. For instance, a toddler isn't ready for a puzzle of more than two or three pieces.

Offer your child open-ended toys. These are toys he can use for more than one type of play. For example, your child can play with paint, blocks, or dolls in many ways. A coloring book, though, has only one use. When the toy is open-ended, children can play with it in many different ways and develop their imaginations.

Babies and toddlers do get tired of the same toys after a while. You can rotate which toys you leave out for them to play with. Bring out the blocks for a few days, then put those away and bring out the pots and pans, followed by the tennis balls, etc. Watch to see what they like best. You'll soon see how long each toy keeps them entertained.

Lots of parents complain that their children ignore the toys they have. One way to deal with this is to get rid of the toy box. It's hard for babies and toddlers to choose a toy that is all jumbled together with others. Display the toys neatly on low shelves or tables. This way your baby or toddler can easily choose what he wants.

Making Throwaways into Toys

Some of the things you ordinarily throw away can be re-made into toys for toddlers. Here are a few ideas.

Save the scoops that come with your laundry detergent. Wash them well. Give them to your toddler to play with in the bathtub or in the sandbox.

Save your old plastic bleach or dishwasher detergent bottles with handles and lids. Wash them well. Cut off the bottom half of the bottle. If the cut edge on the top half is too rough for little hands, tape it with masking or duct tape. Toddlers can use the top half as a funnel in the sandbox or bathtub. Show them how to screw the lid off so the water or sand can pour through. You can also use these as megaphones.

Save the metal lids that come on frozen cans of juice. Wash them. Have your toddler decorate them with stickers. Cut a slit in the top of an empty oatmeal box. Show your toddler how to drop the juice-can lids inside.

Story Time

Make story time with your baby a regular part of your day. It's just as important as playing outside or with blocks. Few things bring parents and children more fun and closeness than reading a favorite story together.

Children get some of the following things from reading with Mom and Dad:

 Learning new words

 A fun chance to cuddle on Mom or Dad's lap

 Practice at sorting out what is real and what is pretend

 Learning about feelings

 Practice at using imagination

 A chance to connect words and pictures

There are thousands of books published each year for young children. Some of them are good and some of them are not. Selecting books from the library, or buying them, is important. How can you choose well?

Here are some points to keep in mind when choosing and reading books to babies and toddlers.

Always read a book yourself first, before reading it to your child.

Be willing to read the same book over and over to your child. She needs time to develop her "favorites."

Go to the library or bookstore regularly. Let your child see where books come from.

 Make sure books are around for your baby or toddler to just pick up and play with. Books are not for keeping high up on a shelf. They are for reading and playing with. Get sturdy cardboard or cloth books if you're worried that she will hurt the books.

Make sure your child sees you having fun reading. She will want to be like you.

Choose books that show children and adults in a balanced way. Children need to see themselves in stories. A little girl will not "see herself" in books showing boys in trains, nor will a Native American child see herself in books that just show Caucasian families. It's good for children to see our many similarities and differences.

Reading with Babies

Very young babies like looking at faces, things they see every day (bottles, shoes, hats, spoons), and other babies. They tend to like color photos better than drawings, though as they grow older, they will like both.

Find sturdy cardboard books, cloth books, or plastic books that babies can chew on and not hurt. It's okay to chew on a book when you're a baby—it's just another way to find out what a book is and what it does.

Read to your baby only as long as he pays attention. If he's done after 45 seconds, go on to some other activity. As babies get older, after about twelve months, they will begin to choose to play with books. By about fifteen months they will be helping you turn pages.

Don't be put off by picture books without words. Look at the pictures with your baby, and name the objects. See if the baby will point to what you name. For example, say, *"Look at that. The daddy is feeding the baby. They look cozy, don't they? Let's turn the page. Where's the baby? That's right! There he is."*

Reading with Toddlers

On-the-move toddlers will often settle down well for a story. They love reading the same book over and over again. Books with just a few words per page hold their attention best. Like older babies, they respond eagerly to rhythm, rhyme, and repetition. Nursery rhymes are very popular with toddlers.

They like books about what is familiar in their own lives: going to bed, playing, eating, or getting dressed. They like books with words or phrases that repeat over and over again.

You can still shorten the text with toddlers (although by age two and a half, you may get strong protests if you skip even one word).

Books to Enjoy

Books for Parents

Here are a few suggestions for books of games and activities to play with babies.

Baby's First Year: Calendar of Learning Games and Memories, Norma Jean Stodden, Ph.D. 1986. International Education Corporation, P.O. Box 89338, Honolulu, HI 96830.

Joyful Play with Toddlers: Recipes for Fun with Odds and Ends, Sandi Dexter. Seattle: Parenting Press, Inc., 1995.

No Bored Babies, Jan Fisher Shea. 1986. Bear Creek Publications, 2507 Minor Ave. E, Seattle, WA 98102.

Books for Babies

Even very young babies love cloth and board books. There are hundreds available. Here are just a couple tried-and-true favorites. Ask your librarian to suggest more.

All Fall Down, Helen Oxenbury. New York: Macmillan Publishing, 1987.

Baby's Favorite Things, Marsha Cohen. New York: Random House, 1986.

Baby's Toys, Grace Maccarone. New York: Scholastic/Avon, 1990.

Clap Hands, Helen Oxenbury. New York: Macmillan Publishing, 1987.

Goodnight, Good Morning, Helen Oxenbury. New York: Penguin Books, 1982.

Max's Bath, Rosemary Wells. New York: Penguin Books, 1985.

1,2,3: A First Book of Numbers, Tana Hoban. New York: Greenwillow Books, 1985.

Pat the Bunny, Dorothy Kunhardt. New York: Golden Press, 1976.

Red, Blue, Yellow Shoe: A First Book of Colors, Tana Hoban. New York: Greenwillow Books, 1986.

Say Goodnight, Helen Oxenbury. New York: Macmillan Publishing, 1987.

Tickle, Tickle, Helen Oxenbury. New York: Macmillan Publishing, 1987.

What Do Babies Do?, Debby Slier. New York: Random House, 1985.

What Is It? A First Book of Objects, Tana Hoban. New York: Greenwillow Books, 1985.

Books for Toddlers

A Dark, Dark Tale, Ruth Brown. New York: Penguin Books, 1981.

Book of Nursery and Mother Goose Rhymes, Marguerite de Angeli. New York: Doubleday, 1954.

Each Peach, Pear, Plum, Janet & Allan Ahlberg. New York: Puffin Books, 1978.

Goodnight Moon, Margaret Wise Brown. New York: Harper & Row, 1947.

Jake Baked the Cake, B. G. Hennessy. New York: Puffin Books, 1990.

Just Like Daddy, Frank Asch. New York: Simon & Schuster, 1981.

Max's Dragon Shirt, Rosemary Wells. New York: Penguin Books, 1991.

Runaway Bunny, Margaret Wise Brown. New York: Harper & Row, 1942.

Sheep in a Jeep, Nancy Shaw. Boston: Houghton Mifflin, 1986.

We're Going On a Bear Hunt, Helen Oxenbury. New York: Macmillan Books, 1989.
Yucky Reptile Alphabet Book, (The), Jerry Pallotta. Watertown, Penn.: Charlesbridge Publishing, 1989.

To find out about more books like these, you can visit your public library or a bookstore. Your librarian and bookseller can direct you to the best books on playing with your child. They can also tell you the best books to read with babies and toddlers.

Use this book often. Have fun and don't stop playing!

Subject Index

Order these books for quick ideas

Tools for Everyday Parenting Series
Illustrated. Paperback, $9.95 each; library binding, $18.95 each

These books are geared for new or frustrated parents. Fun to look at and fun to read, they present information in both words and cartoons. They are perfect for parents who may be busy with school, jobs, or other responsibilities and who have little time to read.

Magic Tools for Raising Kids, by Elizabeth Crary • Parenting young children is easier and more effective with a toolbox of useful, child-tested, positive tools. Learn what to do, how to do it, and what to say to make raising lovable, self-confident kids easier.
128 pages, ISBN 0-943990-77-7 paperback, 0-943990-78-5 library

365 Wacky, Wonderful Ways to Get Your Children to Do What You Want, by Elizabeth Crary • Young children share certain behaviors that are calculated to drive parents crazy. Here are hundreds of practical (and sometimes zany) ideas to help parents cope.
104 pages, ISBN 0-943990-79-3 paperback, 0-943990-80-7 library

More books and ordering information on next page

Order these books for quick ideas

More books on preceding page. Paperback, $9.95 each; library binding $18.95 each

Peekaboo and Other Games to Play with Your Baby, by Shari Steelsmith • Babies love games and this book is full of games they enjoy at different stages of development. All games help develop skills, are fun, and strengthen the bond between baby and parent.
120 pages, ISBN 0-943990-81-5 paperback, 0-943990-99-8 library

Joyful Play with Toddlers: Recipes for Fun with Odds and Ends, by Sandi Dexter • Toddlers at play are full of curiosity and daring. They need creative and safe ways to express themselves. Parents need lots of ideas for no-cost or low-cost toys, games, and activities.
128 pages, ISBN 1-884734-00-6 paperback, 1-884734-01-4 library

Taking Care of Me (So I Can Take Care of Others), by Barbara Carlson, Margaret Healy, Glo Wellman • By taking care of themselves, parents can take care of their children (and others) better. Learn how temperament, childhood experiences, basic needs, and goals affect parenting style.
104 pages, ISBN 1-884734-02-2 paperback, 1-884734-03-0 library

Ask for these books at your favorite bookstore, or call toll free 1-800-992-6657. VISA and MasterCard accepted with phone orders. Complete book catalog available on request.

Parenting Press, Inc., Dept. 501, P.O. Box 75267, Seattle, WA 98125
In Canada, call **Raincoast Books Distribution Co.,** 1-800-663-5714.
Prices subject to change without notice.